Brotherly Feelings

of related interest

Special Brothers and Sisters
Stories and Tips for Siblings of Children with a Disability or Serious Illness
Edited by Annette Hames and Monica McCaffrey
Illustrated by Brendan McCaffrey
ISBN 978 1 84310 383 7

All Cats Have Asperger Syndrome
Kathy Hoopmann
ISBN 978 1 84310 481 0

Do You Understand Me?
My Life, My Thoughts, My Autism Spectrum Disorder
Sofie Koborg Brøsen
ISBN 978 1 84310 464 3

The Complete Guide to Asperger's Syndrome
Tony Attwood
ISBN 978 1 84310 495 7

Asperger's Syndrome
A Guide for Parents and Professionals
Tony Attwood
Foreword by Lorna Wing
ISBN 978 1 84310 577 8

Different Like Me
My Book of Autism Heroes
Jennifer Elder
Illustrations by Marc Thomas and Jennifer Elder
ISBN 978 1 84310 815 3

Baj and the Word Launcher
Space Age Asperger Adventures in Communication
Pamela Victor
Cover illustration by Chris Shadoian
ISBN 978 1 84310 830 6

Brotherly Feelings

Me, My Emotions, and My Brother with Asperger's Syndrome

Sam Frender and Robin Schiffmiller

Illustrations by Dennis Dittrich

Jessica Kingsley Publishers
London and Philadelphia

First published in 2007
by Jessica Kingsley Publishers
116 Pentonville Road
London N1 9JB, UK
and
400 Market Street, Suite 400
Philadelphia, PA 19106, USA

www.jkp.com

Library of Congress Cataloging in Publication Data

Frender, Sam, 1996-
Brotherly feelings : me, my emotions, and my brother with Asperger's syndrome / Sam Frender and Robin Schiffmiller ; illustrations by Dennis Dittrich. -- 1st pbk. ed.
p. cm.
ISBN-13: 978-1-84310-850-4 (pbk. : alk. paper)
ISBN-10: 1-84310-850-X (pbk. : alk. paper) 1. Asperger's syndrome--Juvenile literature. 2. Asperger's syndrome--Patients--Family relationships--Juvenile literature. I. Schiffmiller, Robin, 1957- II. Title.
RJ506.A9B7644 2007
618.92'858832--dc22
2006031696

British Library Cataloguing in Publication Data
A CIP catalogue record for this book is available from the British Library

ISBN 978 1 84310 850 4

Printed and bound in the United States by
Thomson-Shore, Inc.

Contents

A Note for Parents and Professionals

The characters in this book are based on my own sons: Eric (age 13) who has Asperger's Syndrome, and Sam (age 8) who is "neurotypical."

Caring for Eric has always been a full-time job – frequently requiring undivided attention and crisis management. During these stressful times, I have always worried that my lack of immediate focus on Sam might make him feel neglected, unsafe, or even unloved. How many times has he made sacrifices, waited in doctors' offices, or given up play dates or vacation time? How often has he had to watch temper tantrums, or deal with his brother's social awkwardness? I was desperate to know how Sam was feeling.

The goal of this book is to provide the siblings of children with Asperger's Syndrome with an opportunity to explore their feelings and talk about their experiences. It is intended to reassure these children that they are not alone, and to let them know that there are many other children who face similar challenges and have similar feelings. By encouraging our children to articulate their feelings about their siblings, we are better able to understand their concerns, and can become more effective in helping them learn to cope.

As young children become more aware of the world around them, they also become increasingly more aware of the "out of sync" behaviors of their sibling with Asperger's Syndrome. These behaviors, which once elicited their curiosity, compassion, or even amusement, can later cause them feelings of jealousy, resentment and frustration, or even a desire for revenge.

Since siblings will have relationships with each other long after we are gone, it is extremely important for typical siblings to become comfortable with, and accepting of, their Asperger's siblings. Conventional sibling rivalry is tough enough…rivalry with a special needs sibling can be overwhelming. In fact, many of the experiences in this book are not unique to being the sibling of a child with

Asperger's Syndrome, and may be of use to siblings of children with other special needs as well.

The first section of this book describes common characteristics of Asperger's Syndrome in a way that a child will understand. It then goes on to discuss the feelings that neurotypical siblings are likely to experience, at various times, during their relationships with their brother or sister with Asperger's.

The experiences described in the book can be used to help initiate conversations between our children and the many important people in their lives: their brother or sister with Asperger's, their parents, their therapist, plus extended family members or friends. They will also help children explore conflicts within themselves; for example, the loving, yet resentful, feelings they have for their sibling; or the frustrations of being younger, yet feeling more mature.

Acceptance of these feelings helps promote the self-acceptance and self-respect so critical to all children.

If it helps, you can read this book with your neurotypical children. It is not necessary to read the entire book in one sitting. You can pick and choose feelings to read as they become relevant, or read one or two feelings each night. Also, you can refer back to specific feelings over and over again.

Ask your children if they have ever experienced these same feelings. Encourage them to give examples. Perhaps they have feelings which are similar or perhaps the feelings which are described in the book will cause them to think of other feelings.

Ask your children to help Sam solve his problems. What should Sam say to his parents or to his brother in order to help him resolve his feelings? What advice would you give Sam?

By articulating these feelings, siblings of children with Asperger's Syndrome are able to see their brother or sister in a different light, and think about their relationship in a rational and reasoned way. They will feel relieved to know that you are aware of their feelings, that their feelings are legitimate, and that you still love them.

It will also be helpful to read this book with children who have Asperger's Syndrome. Children with Asperger's Syndrome are usually unaware of the impact their behavior has on those around them. Their world is relatively self-centered and self-contained, and the frustrations that can be felt by their sibling rarely enter their thoughts.

This book can be used to initiate conversations with our Asperger's Syndrome children about their relationships with their brother or sister. It can help them begin to understand how their behaviors can affect and influence others. This conversation would need to be approached with care, and would need to be discussed in a way that an Asperger's sibling would be able to understand.

Depending upon the level of sophistication and maturity, the communication may be as simple as "Sam felt sad when his brother broke his toy" or as detailed as the descriptions included in the book.

Children with Asperger's Syndrome also find many social norms hard to comprehend or remember. In order to learn, Asperger's children need to be presented with these concepts multiple times.

In explaining their feelings to their brother or sister with Asperger's, typical siblings may have to repeat their feelings over and over again. As a family you can refer back to specific feelings in the book as often as needed. As the children develop and mature, the content of these conversations will change and expand, as will the relationships between the siblings.

So often, extended families and close friends do not truly understand the experiences of a family living with Asperger's Syndrome. This book provides an opportunity to share feelings with uncles, aunts, and grandparents in a non-threatening way. It may also offer them an opportunity to share feelings that they have too. By reading the book, family members will understand a great deal more about your children and your family relationships.

Professionals working with children can use this book in a similar way – to gain an insight into the family's relationships as well as into the feelings of our children.

Writing this book has been therapeutic for everyone in our family. We refer to it often and we draw strength from it. We hope that you will too!

Robin Schiffmiller (Sam and Eric's mom)

Note From Sam

My name is Sam.
I am 8 years old.
I have a brother who is 13 years old.
His name is Eric.

He has Asperger's Syndrome.

I am writing this book because I want other kids to know
what it feels like to live with a sibling
who has Asperger's Syndrome.

I have lots of different feelings about Eric.
I show him these feelings in my face,
with my body, and with my voice...
but he doesn't always seem to understand them,
or know how to respond, when I communicate them.

I love Eric very much.

I can't imagine life without him...
but life with him is sometimes tough.

I know that there are other kids out there
who have siblings with Asperger's.
I thought it would be nice to share our experiences.
That way, we wouldn't feel so alone.

I know that all people are different,
and not all big brothers with Asperger's behave the same way.
But I hope that, by sharing my own experiences and feelings,
I will help YOU!

What is Asperger's Syndrome?

Asperger's Syndrome changes the way somebody's brain works. It can be a little different for every person that has it, so I can only tell you what it's like for Eric.

For Eric, having Asperger's Syndrome means that he needs more time than you or I do to think about a question before he answers it. Even though he may have the answer in his brain, it takes him longer to find it.

It means that he has a hard time making friends his own age, because he doesn't really get some of the "cool" things that kids his age say and do.

It means that he has a hard time doing more than one thing at a time. If he is listening to you, he will have a hard time looking at you; or if you ask him to do two things at the same time, he will get confused and not know which one to do first.

It means that he has one special thing that he likes more than everything else in the world. He knows a lot about his special thing and he talks about it all the time. He talks about it so much that sometimes other people get tired of hearing about it.

It means that he feels overwhelmed by simple everyday things. Sometimes, he feels so overwhelmed that he will scream and cry. Sometimes, when he's screaming and crying, he doesn't even remember who he is or why he is crying. It is almost like he has another person who lives inside him and takes over his body.

It means that he worries about everything. He worries that he will be late or that he will forget something. He worries that I will get hurt while I am playing, or that my glass of milk might fall off the edge of the table. He worries that his hair isn't neat enough, or that he won't know what to say if someone speaks to him.

It means that he has a hard time paying attention and concentrating. School is very hard for him...and homework is even harder. If Mom asks him to take a shower, he will find a toy along the way and start playing with it. He forgets all about the shower. You have to constantly remind him.

It means that he is super-sensitive to everything around him. Crowds and loud noises make him uncomfortable. He hates the way certain foods feel on his tongue or the way certain fabrics feel on his skin. He tears the labels out of all his clothes. He doesn't like to be touched—unless he's in the mood. And he notices the way everything smells—even the inside of houses and cars.

But most of all, I think that for Eric, having Asperger's can mean feeling lonely. I think he sometimes feels like a puzzle piece that doesn't quite fit the puzzle. It looks like it should fit...but it just doesn't.

This is what Asperger's feels like for my brother.

What are Feelings?

Feelings are hard to describe. They are thoughts, inside of us, that affect the way we behave. Sometimes we know what our feelings are...and sometimes we know we feel something, but we can't give the feeling a name.

There are so many feelings that you can't even name them all. You can feel **happy** when you are playing with your friend, **disappointed** if you missed your favorite TV show, **excited** when you are about to open a present, or **nervous** when you are about to try something for the first time. The list of feelings goes on forever.

Everyone has feelings...lots of feelings. In fact, people can even have more than one feeling at the same time. If you've ever been on a roller coaster, you probably felt both **nervous** and **excited**! Or if your mom hugs you in front of your friends you might feel **loved**...but also a little **embarrassed**!

There is no such thing as a right feeling or a wrong feeling.

All feelings are OK!

They can come in all shapes and sizes. We can have feelings that last for only a few seconds, like being **surprised** when someone says, "boo!" Or we can have feelings that last for a long time, like feeling **lonely** when our best friend moves away.

Sometimes we hardly notice our feelings, and other times they can change the way our bodies feel. If we feel **nervous**, our hearts may race or we may feel tingly or sweaty. If we feel **sad**, we may cry. If we feel **happy**, we may laugh.

Some feelings drag other feelings along with them. When I feel **angry, frustrated**, or **jealous**, I sometimes end up feeling **guilty** too. I end up thinking that I am a bad person for having these feelings, and that no one should like me. Other times, these kinds of feelings make me feel overwhelmed, because it feels like there are little volcanoes inside of me...just waiting to explode.

Sometimes feelings can get stuck inside of us. When they do, the best thing to do is let them out. Once they come out, they seem easier to understand and easier to live with. If they are bothersome feelings, they seem to bother us less once we say them out loud.

I had a lot of feelings stuck inside of me. I wrote this book so I could let all those feelings come out. Once they came out...I felt so much better. It felt so good not to have them stuck inside of me anymore.

Maybe when you read about my feelings, you will find feelings that are stuck inside of you. If you can talk to your parents about these stuck feelings, you might be able to let them out. Once they come out, I bet you will feel a lot better!

My Feelings

I used to feel...Doomed

I sometimes worried that I would grow up to be like my brother Eric. I didn't understand why he behaved the way he did. I was afraid that I could catch his problems.

Now I understand that my brother and I are different. We each face our own challenges and have our own strengths.

Sometimes I feel...Afraid

I get scared when Eric has temper tantrums. He says things like "I hate you!" He screams and curses and throws things.

My mom and I made up a safe place for me to go when he is having a tantrum. I go in my mom's room and I lock the door.

My mom wrote family and emergency phone numbers on the back of all the phones in the house. Now, if I feel scared, I can call someone while my mom is busy keeping Eric safe, during his tantrum.

Afraid

Sometimes I feel...Annoyed

Sometimes Eric has a tantrum when it is time to do his homework, take a bath, clean his room, or practice his music. I have to do these things too. They aren't so hard. I don't understand why he has to make such a big deal about simple everyday things. It is so annoying.

Sometimes I feel...Protective

Eric gets very nervous around people he doesn't know. When he gets nervous, he doesn't know what to say or do. Sometimes he just stands there looking a little scared.

When he gets scared, he has tics. Tics are movements he makes with his body. Sometimes he shakes his head. Sometimes he sniffs or coughs a lot. Sometimes he throws things up in the air. And sometimes he picks at his skin or cuts his clothes.

My family is used to his tics, but most kids don't understand why he does them. They think it is weird. Not only do they not want to be his friend, but they also tease him and bully him.

I wish that I were with Eric when this happens. I am not afraid of other kids. I would tell them to cut it out. I would help Eric feel safe.

Even when I was very young I felt that I needed to protect Eric. He would frequently cause mischief around the house. He was always getting himself into trouble. It made me feel so sad to see him being scolded. I knew he couldn't help what he was doing—and that he didn't do bad things on purpose. So, to protect him, I would take the blame for things that Eric did wrong. I would tell my family that I did it. For many years I accepted the

Protective

consequences and punishments of my brother's inappropriate behaviors. Once I got older, though, I understood that my parents needed to know the truth. Now I tell my parents when Eric does something wrong—even if telling makes me feel bad.

Sometimes I feel...Overwhelmed

I'm just a little guy, but everyone asks me to be understanding and patient with Eric. Sometimes it's just too much for me. I just want to be a regular kid with a regular brother and a regular family. Sometimes I wish I could just go to live with a different family, or stay in a hotel...just to get away from it all.

Sometimes I feel...Disappointed

When I was younger, my mom would say I was too young to do certain things by myself. She would only let me do them if Eric went with me.

However, Eric would sometimes forget why he was going along. He would become interested in something else and forget to keep an eye on me.

Even though he is five years older than me, Mom had to stop asking Eric to watch me. Other kids get to do things alone with their big brothers. I wish I could too.

Overwhelmed

Sometimes I feel...Worried

Eric can't always control his behavior. I worry that my brother will have a bad life. I am afraid that he will get into trouble. I worry that he will get hurt, or maybe hurt someone else.

Sometimes I feel...Bothered

Eric is very funny and he likes to act silly a lot of the time. I usually enjoy watching him be silly. He makes me laugh. But sometimes I have to concentrate. And sometimes I just don't feel silly. I ask him to stop, but he doesn't. I know he can't help it, but it really gets on my nerves!

Other times, Eric will come into my room while I am still sleeping and he will wake me up. He knows that I am sleeping, but he wants to be with me. I know that he feels lonely without me, so I don't want to get mad at him, but I really hate it when he wakes me up.

It's even hard sometimes when Eric just wants to show me he loves me. He likes to hug me or give me a kiss. I love him too, but sometimes it bothers me the way he shows his love: he hugs me too tight, or gives me slobbery kisses. Mom tries to teach him how to be gentle, but he just doesn't seem to get it.

Worried

Sometimes I feel...Impatient

It always takes a long time to get ready to go someplace when Eric comes along. He can never leave the house without certain toys that he likes to carry with him.

It doesn't matter how late we are, he has to find the toys he needs. If he can't find them he can end up having a tantrum. Sometimes I run out of patience.

Sometimes I feel...Guilty

There are times when Eric's behavior makes me so upset, that I feel like I don't love him anymore. Once I told him how I felt. It made him very sad.

The next morning I felt so guilty about my feelings, that I hated myself. I couldn't live with the idea that I didn't love him anymore. I wanted to hurt myself.

Impatient

Sometimes I feel...Mischievous

If Eric gets on my nerves, sometimes I want revenge. I will try to get him into trouble by telling my parents that he did something that he didn't really do. I know it's not right. Sometimes I just can't help it.

Sometimes I feel...Resentful

I know that Eric needs special help, but sometimes I resent that he gets to do special things even though he misbehaves. I don't think he deserves it.

Mom and Dad are always taking Eric to doctors. I spend a lot of time in waiting rooms. It is very boring. I can't play with my friends or do the things that I want to do.

Sometimes I even feel resentful that Mom and Dad spend lots of money to get help for Eric, because it means that we don't have money left for fun things like vacations. I wish everything in life were free!

Mischievous

Sometimes I feel...Embarrassed

Eric likes to dress up like his favorite TV characters and to carry the things they use on the show. He always wants me to play along, which is fine when we are at home. But I feel silly when he wants me to do it in public, like at the mall, or in the supermarket.

I am too old to be doing these kinds of things. I worry that someone will make fun of me. I usually do it anyway, though, because I love him

Sometimes I don't want to talk to my friends about Eric because I am embarrassed to tell them about the things that he does. I am afraid that people in my school will know that he is my brother, and they will think that I will behave the way he does, and they won't want to be my friends.

Sometimes I feel...Suspicious

Sometimes I assume that Eric is guilty of doing something wrong even if I don't have proof. Since he often does bad things, I accuse him when I find something broken in my room...even if I don't know, for sure, that he did it.

Suspicious

Sometimes I feel...Lonely

Even though Eric bothers me sometimes, I miss him very much when he is gone. I enjoy being away from him for a couple of hours, but I don't like it when he is away for a long time.

Sometimes I feel like I am the only kid who has to deal with this kind of stuff. That makes me feel lonely too.

Sometimes I feel...Sloppy

I am lucky enough to have my own bedroom, but I do share a bathroom with Eric. I like to keep my things neat, but being neat is hard for my brother.

In our bathroom, he forgets to put his dirty clothes in the hamper or his trash in the garbage pail, and he leaves toothpaste on the floor and on the counter.

When he is nervous or angry, he cuts holes in the towels or shower curtain and pulls the towel bar and paint off the walls. I try to keep the room clean, but it really isn't possible. I like to be neat and organized. The messy bathroom bothers me.

Sometimes I feel...Confident

I figure that if Eric can accomplish all that he does with Asperger's, imagine what I can accomplish without it. Sometimes I feel like I can help people. Sometimes I feel like I can change the world.

Confident

Sometimes I feel...Misled

Eric finds small, everyday problems very hard to deal with. When he started school, he found it very hard to change from one activity to another, and homework was terrifying for him. He would cry and scream every night.

When it was my turn to go to school, I wanted no part of it. I thought school was an evil place; after all, it made Eric cry everyday.

I refused to go to kindergarten and I hated first grade. Now that I am in second grade, I finally realize that I really like school. School is not hard for me like it is for Eric. Now I can relax and enjoy it.

Sometimes I feel...Doubtful

When Eric is in a bad mood, he sometimes takes it out on me. When he finally realizes that it's not me that he's mad at, he usually apologizes.

But his apologies are often hard to believe. For one thing, he never looks at me when he apologizes, and for another, his voice doesn't sound like he really means it. He says he's sorry, but it's hard to believe him.

Doubtful

Sometimes I feel...Relieved

Since everybody's Asperger's looks different, sometimes it's hard to know when someone has it. It took a very long time for my mom and dad to figure out that Eric had Asperger's.

I kept worrying about Eric and getting upset about his behavior. My parents would tell me that they were trying to help my brother and that I should be patient. I hated being patient. It seemed like nothing ever changed and nothing ever got better.

First doctors told my mom that my brother was very nervous; then that he had trouble concentrating; then that he changed moods too often and then that he misbehaved on purpose. They gave him medicine for each of these things, but Eric never got better.

Finally, they found out that Eric had Asperger's. They said it was hard to find out because there were a lot of things about my brother that didn't look like Asperger's.

You can't make Asperger's go away. There is no medicine that will cure Eric. But, now that we all know what is wrong with him, we can help him be the best he can be. We can help him be happy. I am so relieved!

Sometimes I feel...Puzzled

I can't figure out why Eric behaves the way he does. I try to come up with different reasons, like: maybe he is hanging out with bad kids and learning bad behaviors from them, maybe the medicine is wrong, maybe there is something wrong with his brain, or maybe he's just mean. I never really know for sure.

Puzzled

Sometimes I feel...Frustrated

Eric doesn't have many friends. He feels more comfortable with my friends than with kids his own age. When my friends come over, he tries to play with them and he ends up taking them away from me.

When Eric does have a friend come over, he won't let me play. He is afraid I might take his friend away and he wants the friend all to himself. He wants me to share my friends, but he doesn't want to share his.

When I do play with Eric, he likes to make up all the rules of the game. He likes to decide what everyone is going to do and say and he wants everything to be his way. It's very frustrating.

Eric also has a lot of nice toys. He is supposed to pass these toys to me when he gets too old for them. But many of these toys do not last long enough for me to play with. Eric will take them apart. Sometimes he uses pieces of the toys to make something. Sometimes he takes them apart just because he feels like it. He always seems to take apart the cool stuff.

I would like to be rich one day, so I can buy everything I want. That way, it won't matter what he breaks!

Frustrated

Sometimes I feel...Invaded

Eric does things without thinking. He also has a hard time remembering not to do certain things, even though we tell him many times.

He likes to go in my room without permission. He likes to take things that belong to me. Sometimes he comes in my room and throws things around and makes my room very messy. Sometimes he breaks my things by accident, and sometimes he breaks them on purpose.

I am not allowed to go into Eric's room without permission. I follow that rule. Eric doesn't let me touch his toys. I don't mess up his room, and I don't break his toys. It doesn't seem fair.

Sometimes I feel...Sad

I feel sad that Eric's life is so hard for him. I wish he had more friends. I wish school were easier for him. I wish he didn't have to have tantrums. I wish he could be happy more of the time.

Invaded

Sometimes I feel...Bored

Eric likes to do the same things over and over again. He likes to watch the same TV show, listen to the same songs, and play the same games. If he says or does something to make you laugh, he will keep doing it even after it isn't funny anymore. He never seems to know when to stop.

Even though I enjoy playing with Eric, I get bored doing the same things all the time.

Sometimes I feel...Sick

Sometimes my feelings about my brother are in my body instead of in my mind. When things get rough, I can get headaches and stomach aches.

I go to the doctor, but she doesn't find anything wrong with me. My mom says it's stress, so we practice being calm.

Bored

Sometimes I feel...Hurt

When Eric's behavior is out of control he sometimes hurts me. He can hurt me by the things he says and by the things he does.

When he is having a tantrum, he will say mean and horrible things to me. He tells me that he hates me, that I'm stupid, that he wishes he didn't have a little brother. These mean words hurt my feelings and make me feel very sad, even though my mom reminds me that he doesn't really mean what he is saying.

When Eric and I play, he can get very excited and make the game too rough or too wild for me. When he gets this way, sometimes I get hurt. It upsets me, even though I know he didn't mean it.

Sometimes I feel...Babied

Even though I am not a baby anymore, Eric still treats me like one. He is always telling me to be careful of this or watch out for that. He tries to help me even when I don't need help. He tries to talk for me and do things for me.

He also likes to describe things perfectly. If I am telling a story, he corrects me if I don't tell every detail the same way he would tell it.

I can take care of myself and I can speak for myself. I wish he would stop.

Hurt

Sometimes I feel...Interrupted

There are times when my mom and dad are talking just with me: maybe they are helping me with my homework, or maybe we are reading, or maybe I am telling them about my day in school.

Well, Eric will come in and start talking to my parents as though I were not even there. Even if Mom and Dad tell him that they are busy and he has to wait, he keeps right on talking. He thinks everything he has to say is very important and he is worried that he will forget what he wants to say.

Sometimes I feel...Optimistic

I feel good when Eric is nice to me and does kind things. I think that maybe he has changed and I start to trust him. Sometimes he does his homework or takes a shower without complaining. Then I think that maybe he will be all right after all.

Interrupted

Sometimes I feel...Angry

Eric's uncontrollable behavior is very upsetting to my mom and dad. They try to be patient, but sometimes they yell, and sometimes they even cry.

I get very angry with Eric when he upsets my parents. It makes the whole family unhappy.

Sometimes I feel...Innocent

Sometimes when my mom and dad get upset with Eric, they take it out on me. They don't mean to, but once they are upset it is hard for them to calm down. So I get yelled at, even if I didn't do anything. I hate that!

Angry

Sometimes I feel...Pressured

Since Eric's behavior upsets my mom and dad and I don't want them to be unhappy, I often feel that I should be perfect so they will be happy. I feel that I can't make mistakes or do anything wrong because they will end up being even more upset.

For example, my brother only likes to eat certain foods. If my dad cooks something new, Eric does not want to taste it. Sometimes he will have a tantrum if someone asks him to eat something he doesn't think he will like. It can ruin the whole dinner.

I feel like I have to eat everything my dad makes and say "it's great!" even if I don't really like it. I don't want my dad to feel hurt or upset.

Even though my mom and dad tell me that no one is perfect and that I don't have to fix the family's problems, I still feel that I have to do it.

Trying to be perfect is very exhausting.

Pressured

Sometimes I feel...Responsible

I spend even more time with Eric than Mom and Dad do. Since he doesn't always think about what he's doing, I always feel that I have to watch him to make sure that he's OK.

It's hard to have fun while you are worrying about someone else. Sometimes I feel like I'm the older brother even though I'm not.

Sometimes I feel...Unimpressive

Since Eric has so many problems, people make a big deal about his accomplishments.

Sometimes I feel like my accomplishments don't get as much attention as they should. My challenges are just as hard for me as his are for him. Why don't mine seem to impress everyone as much?

Unimpressive

Sometimes I feel...Compassionate

Deep down inside, I know that Eric can't always stop his bad behavior. I know he doesn't do it on purpose. I know that he feels scared when he is out of control, and I know that he regrets saying mean things to me.

So, no matter what Eric says or does, I always forgive him. I always still love him.

Sometimes I feel...Needed

Eric once said that without his family he would be nothing. I am an important member of the family. Having me as his brother is a part of who he is. My brother needs me. I need him too.

Sometimes I feel...Happy

Eric can make me laugh so hard that I can't breathe. I have a lot of fun playing with him.

Needed

Sometimes I feel...Loved

I can tell that Eric really loves me. When I cry he tries anything and everything he can think of to make me happy. He brings me stuffed animals and acts silly to make me laugh.

He wants to spend time with me. He likes to remind me of fun times that we've had. We retell things that make us laugh, over and over again.

He waits for me when I'm busy and he likes to pick me up from the school bus. He takes me for rides on his skateboard and will pull me in a wagon. He tries to get me interested in things that are important to him.

Eric will help me find things when I lose them. He always knows where I am and what I am doing. He worries if I am not where he expects me to be. In his own way, he watches out for me and tries to take care of me.

He loves me.

Sometimes I feel...Proud

Eric has a lot of talents. He makes me laugh. He is very smart. He is a talented musician. He is creative and imaginative.

Even though life is a challenge for him, he never stops trying. He never gives up and he works hard.

I look up to Eric. I am proud of him.

Loved

What I Do When I Can't Take It Anymore!

Sometimes I...Meltdown

OK, I admit it, sometimes I just can't deal with it: I scream, I cry, and I threaten to run away.

I try to tell my mom what I am feeling, but I can't always find the words—and sometimes, she's just not listening.

Other times I don't even realize what's bothering me. I will cry about homework, or dinner, or anything at all, because I am so frustrated that I feel like I'm going to explode.

I really hate feeling this way, but sometimes you just can't help it!

Sometimes I...Get away from it

When Eric gets on my nerves, I try to ignore his behavior and walk away. I know he doesn't have many friends, and that he relies on me for company, but sometimes I just want to be alone or play with someone without his taking over the game. When I

leave him out he feels hurt. I don't mean to hurt him. I just need time without him.

When I need to get away, I go to my room and listen to music, read a book, do arts and crafts or play on the computer. I concentrate on anything that takes my mind off things.

Sometimes I meditate. I close my eyes and concentrate on my breathing. I relax my body and calm down. I try to let everything go out of my mind.

If none of these things work, I go outside or go to a friend's house. I always feel better when I come back.

Sometimes I...Remind myself of the good things

My mom and I made a list of all the things my family does to show me how much they love me. I keep this list on the refrigerator so I can look at it whenever I feel neglected or unloved.

Sometimes when you are frustrated, it is hard to see the good side of things. My list helps me remember all the good things too.

Sometimes I...Talk about it

When things aren't going well at home I try to talk about it. I talk to adults that I trust, like my parents or a therapist.

When I feel neglected or frustrated, Mom or Dad makes special plans to take me out all by myself. I like to go to the mall to walk around, go out to dinner or just go out for ice cream. After I have had time alone with Mom or Dad, I always feel better.

I also talk to Eric. I let him know how I feel so that we can work things out together.

I especially like to talk to other kids who have siblings with autism. It's nice to know that I am not alone.

Sometimes I...Write things down

Sometimes, if I am having mean feelings, I write them in my journal instead of saying them out loud. This way I don't hurt anybody's feelings. When I write my feelings down, I usually feel better.

Sometimes I...Learn more about Asperger's

I am always asking questions about Asperger's and autism. If my mom goes to a class, I ask her what she learned. She and I read books together about Asperger's.

Also, whenever my mom learns something new, she tells me about it. By learning more about Asperger's, I can understand my brother better.

When I understand Eric and his behavior better, I find it less upsetting and easier to be around him.

Letting My Feelings Out

As you can see, I had a lot of feelings stuck inside me. I worried about them a lot. Sometimes I thought that the feelings were bad, and that I was a bad person for having them.

I was so relieved to find out that my family still loved me even after I said my feelings out loud. They told me that all my feelings were acceptable...and they meant it.

Eric still loves me, even though I told him that sometimes his behavior makes me feel angry or resentful. My mom and dad still love me even though I told them that sometimes I feel jealous or mischievous.

Now, when I have a strong feeling about something, I say it out loud to my mom, dad or my brother. When I talk about the feeling right away, it doesn't seem to get stuck inside...and if it does, I just keep talking about it until it comes out.

Having a brother with Asperger's can be tough. Everyday Eric and I grow up a little, and everyday we have different experiences. Since our lives are constantly changing...our feelings change too.

Each time we have new feelings, we need to talk about them. Each time we talk about them, we get closer and have a better relationship. I think we will keep talking about our feelings forever!

A Final Note From Sam

I want to thank my mom
for helping me put my ideas down on paper.
It really helps me to know that my family
is listening to me,
and that they know how I feel.

I read my book to Eric.
I was afraid that my feelings might have made him angry.
There were a few times I could see
that he was upset about what I said.

When he was finished
he said that it was hard to read about himself,
but he was smiling.
He told me that he liked my book.
He told me that I did a good job.
I felt proud.